T0333417

THE SEASONS OF CULLEN CHURCH

BERNARD O'DONOGHUE

The Seasons of Cullen Church

FABER & FABER

First published in 2016
by Faber & Faber Ltd
Bloomsbury House
74–77 Great Russell Street
London WC1B 3DA
This paperback edition first published in 2019

Typeset by Hamish Ironside
Printed in England by TJ International Ltd, Padstow, Cornwall

A CIP record for this book is available from the British Library

ISBN 978–0–571–33047–8

2 4 6 8 10 9 7 5 3 1

for Leonard, Nancy and Joseph

Acknowledgements

Eight of these poems were published in a de luxe volume made by Joe McCann at Four Candles Press in Oxford, entitled *Early & Late*. 'Migration' was published in *1914: Poetry Remembers*, edited by Carol Ann Duffy (London: Faber & Faber). 'Specific Gravity' was published in *20/12: Twenty Irish Poets Respond to Science in Twelve Lines*, edited by Iggy McGovern (Dublin: Dedalus Press). 'The Dark Room' was published in *Peter Fallon: Poet, Publisher, Editor and Translator*, edited by R. R. Russell (Sallins: Irish Academic Press). 'At the Hallé' was published in *On Shakespeare's Sonnets*, edited by Hannah Crawforth and Elizabeth Scott-Baumann. 'The Seasons of Cullen Church' was published in *The Church of the Nativity of Mary in Cullen*, edited by Eileen O'Connor (Kanturk: IRD, Duhallow). I am very grateful to the editors of the following publications where some of the poems were published: *Ambit, Archipelago, The Clifden Anthology* (edited by Brendan Flynn), *Cork Literary Review, Dark Horse, Irish Times, New Statesman, Oxford Poetry, P N Review, Poetry Ireland Review, Poetry Review, The Reader, The Spectator, Times Literary Supplement* and *The Yeats Journal of Korea*.

Contents

THE SEASONS OF CULLEN CHURCH

Poverty, though bitter, is most miserable in this –
that it makes men ridiculous.

– JUVENAL, *Satire 3*

Waiting for the Horses

for Keith Hanley

So wistful is the recognition now
of all the places that I hardly noted:
places I know I saw once or twice,
their occasions unrecallable,
like a green caravan in a field-corner.

This year snow lays on the hills already
in mid-November by the northern Lakes
as the train gathers speed up the gradient.
By a level-crossing gate a boy stands,
holding a horse's tackling on his shoulder.

What distant sound does he hear along the tracks?

I don't think I will go by train again.

The Will

When they discovered that my grandfather
was going, unexpectedly, to die young
of meningitis, they naturally set about
ensuring that his wife would not inherit
the farm. They assembled a group of solid men –
as they might have for the threshing: his brother
who lived south on the mountain;
a shrewd solicitor; and a man from Doon
with a good hand who often testified to wills.

There was another witness whose existence
I know from no other evidence: my father's
Uncle Michael. I suppose he emigrated
to the States or Canada, where – I suppose again –
he was set upon at his arrival
for the few pounds sewn inside his coat
and dumped into the sea, or maybe shunned
because of the disease he carried
and left to die in the plague sheds of Grosse Île.

Mahogany Gaspipes

for Pat Palmer

She trembled as she heard again her mother's voice
saying constantly with foolish insistence: –
Derevaun Seraun! Derevaun Seraun!
– JAMES JOYCE, 'Eveline'

They didn't seem to hear what we were saying
across the water: probably the wind
was in the wrong direction and blew away
our voices. But they scrutinised the sounds,
every vocable, to see whether they might
make some sense of them. They suspected jokes,
even when there weren't jokes, and they marvelled
at the inventive twists and turns
and contortedness of this warbling tongue.

Not that we didn't try to name names –
Jula, Willam – or give good directions:
to get to the Bocára where Diarmuid fled
with Gráinne, go straight at Clampers Cross;
you must turn in at Keale bridge
to reach the far side of the causeway
at the Bowing, where the O'Keeffes set their dogs
on O'Sullivan Beare during his Long Walk.
And even we don't know what the Canádas means.

So yes, it has to be conceded that we were
speaking in tongues: that any wisps of meaning
had to be caught while they were flying
to make some sense out of this local parlance.

The Din Beags

Childless all three: the nearest thing
to progeny was a young brother
that snow and lime blinded at Christmas
forty years ago. So now they lived
on courtesy, nice to each other
as unrivalling siblings are.

But, even having so little, there was room
to have less. Robin, the orange mare
with the white star on her brow, loved them
across the gate. Tragedy, then,
when they found her grotesquely dead
one winter morning, teeth drawn back
as if in hate, legs straightened out, rigid.

Although it was just November,
the ground was already too hard
to dig, so they sent for the most vigorous
and carefree man in the townland.
Willingly he picked and shovelled through
the pencil-stone rigid from early frosts.
After three hours the grave was finished
and he lugged the big carcass towards it.
But the hind legs still stuck out, no matter
how he pushed. 'Bring me the Bushman',
he said. 'We can saw the legs off
and throw them in with her.'

The sisters cried and the brother said:
'Leave our fields, and never stand in them again.'
For four hours more they toiled themselves,
chipping at the hard edges till Capella
shone a fierce blue to the north,
before Robin toppled finally
into her duly ordered place of rest.

Ballybeg Priory

for Brian Friel

Writing from Lisbon in 1705,
the Bishop of Cloyne lamented how
'oxen and asses ruminate
under the shadows of the Austins' church
at Ballybeg, the stone coffins of the monks
their watering troughs, and the tombs
where rest the bones of abbots are their byres'.

By now you might expect to find in place
an instructive interpretative centre,
explaining how the columbarium
provided guano which the friars sold
as fertiliser because it was better
for herb gardens and cloth making
than the droppings of the farming stock.

But there are no display cases here:
no art-objects or explanations.
The close is untended, and the walls
go on crumbling. And in the field around
are tinkers' ponies: piebald, skewbald,
ungroomed, unshorn, stumbling blindly
on their overgrown, unfarriered hooves.

The Republic

Our *Concise Oxford English Dictionary*
smells of cigarette smoke still because
Martin le Vay gave it to our children
when he turned against it. All he cared about
was books, but periodically
he'd rebel and give them all away
to friends or passers-by. To explain
this policy he wrote a poet's memoir,
a million words in length, and left it,
where I suppose it remains, under lock and key
in the National Westminster Bank,
five years now after his death.

But when he banished books from the republic
of his head, with its strict rules and regulations
and depressions, he never lost a word
the way we others do. In the early hours,
he smoked and planned what he would write
when the sun had risen and the rain had stopped,
and the words stood ready at his beck and call
to join in with the charm of earliest birds.

Migration

Ledwidge was busy the day before he died,
building a lakeside road like the back road
along the Boyne to Swynnerton from Slane.

The fowler came at break of day, and took him
from his song. The words in his head as he worked –
merle or ouzel or *lon dubh* – exploded in him.
He could not stand aside while others fought
to guard old Ireland's freedom. So he said.

There was no fence or gatepost by that road
to which he could have pinned whatever lines
might cross his mind before the short night came.

Our complement of native blackbirds
are reinforced in winter by battalions
that fly down the North Sea and Baltic
to escape the cold and then join up
with the first February chorus of the spring.

At the Funeral in Oxford of Darky Finn

With the Horseface Toole I knew the rule:
No money if you stop for rain.
   – DOMINIC BEHAN, 'McAlpine's Fusiliers'

The rain battered on the corrugated roof
of the Simon Community while the priest
of the mission to the homeless raised the host
and praised Darky by name. Mick Henry sang –
his voice rising clean through the drumming
on the roof – the ageless Quaker hymn
'How Can I Keep from Singing?'

Way down on the Isle of Grain in days gone by
the sun beating hard on raw shoulders.
High upon the scaffold's eminence
they'd whistle at the girls stalking past.

Now the only other sound through the squall
was the train accelerating from the station,
heading for London. When we came out
it was easing off: 'It might clear up
properly in a while', somebody said,
and someone else said 'We'll be lucky!'

Stigma

*The voice is the voice of Jacob, but the hands
are the hands of Esau.*

– GENESIS 27:22

When Con came to work on the farm for us
his annual wages were one hundred
and twenty pounds, which everybody said
was far too much: more than twice
what Norry had been paid just five years back
before she escaped to America
to marry Tom, her 'swell guy from Mayo'.

But for Con and all his feckless family
it was not enough; often his mother
would come into view along the road
in the donkey-car, to sub from his earnings,
which would not, the agreement was, be paid
until Christmas Eve, when he would get
ten days off. His money consequently

was more than half used up by June. But why
do I keep on returning to that time –
to Con's shaky bike and his one pair
of sandals in which he trudged gaily
through the cow dung? To his reckless nights
in the pub which made it torture for him
to wake for the cows at 6 a.m., clawing

the sleep out of his eyes? Why not stay
with the poverties of our present time:
beggars on bridges for us to trip on,
or asylum seekers loping through
the infra-red at detention centres
on the coast of France, or drowning
in their hundreds in the Med?

The Inseminators

i.m. Bill Neenan

They always sped away too fast
in Prefect, Volks or Dauphine,
in fine summers whipping up a cloud
of white road-dust that penetrated
everything, leaving the farmers to call
them 'Scamps!' But it's no wonder
they wanted to get well clear
of the scene of the crime, with the long
rubber gloves they hauled to the elbow
and secreted deep in the car boot:
a chief surgeon in the docudrama
who had to grope to find the glass pipette
they'd forced into the cow's unprivate parts
that we evaded with the soft term 'dairying'.

The Pay-Off

Sister Una

Those hands that were foresworn
to be only the manipulative
servants of Christ, rooted and tugged
deep in last winter's cow dung
to pull out fertiliser
for next June's ageless roses
in our suburban garden.

Meanwhile I, through no deserving
on my part, have just about escaped
with my hands clean. So I might, with luck,
get away with a medium term –
say seven centuries – in Purgatory,
while she shines, dirt under her nails,
in the highest height of Heaven.

Ganesh

They call me wise, even some kind of god,
and they prostrate themselves in front of me.
But how is it that the busy ant is not
shackled by the foreleg and the hind leg,
that he's not tramping to and fro, fro and to,
unable to see why he can't walk on?

First Night There

Always the same: when you've left your stuff
in the hotel room and taken to the streets,
wondering who you'll find, there is no one.
Where is the crowd? No one in the bars
or walking by the sea: no one back
in the hotel foyer mausoleum.
You know by morning it will be all right:
you'll have found them and made arrangements
for the day: too many encounters
and too many things to do. But still
there will be the tremor of the memory
of the dark evening when you had to people
the whole empty lifescape on your own.

Tsunami

Sometimes I go before people notice
under the waves' rage to seek out the depths,
the plains of the sea-king. He, aroused,
sends the white foam rolling. The whale-lake howls,
roars at its loudest; tide hammers shores;
stones and sand, seaweed and salt-wave
batter in turn the slopes of the cliffs,
when I start fighting, cloaked by the sea,
disturbing the earth and the ocean alike.
Nor am I able to break the sea's cover
before that is granted by him who is master
on all of my travels. You are a wise man:
say who draws me from the depth of the ocean
when the tide grows calmer again
and the waves turn to melody, so deafening before.

Exeter Book, Riddle 2

The Move

My quiet love has moved houses.
Where she is now, the only door
is in the roof and always shut.
One spring and summer after she moved in,
and the thatch was covered with grass.
No one knocks any longer
to ask how she likes her new house
or how she has arranged her sweet furniture.

from the Middle English

Underfoot

The Irish lettering on the slate nameplate
of Umeraboy National School was plastered in
during the War – they told us – so passing spies
would not be helped in finding out their way.
Now it lies flat at the entrance where cars
edge through the cast-iron gates. Some people
see this as an honour, to be laid down
in such prominence, like the rune stones
set on the threshold by the north door
of Gotland churches. Others call it
disrespectful, to place it on the road
where every wheel runs over it, as Man Friday
seized his master's ankle to place his foot
on his own head which he bowed down to the ground.

Riddle

I share my name with the unproductive bees
who do all the work. I travel in the night,
like angels or figments of imagination.
I suffer power cuts, but still perform
my silent ministry. Blind as a worm,
ignorantly butting forward,
I can't be expected to distinguish
weddings from funerals. Gone by morning,
no man knows why. Are your ears burning?
Is someone walking on your grave, once again
imploring you to ask the question
you've always shrunk from asking?

American Night

All in the half-dark, we watch the dead
playing the parts of the living, in roles
we have seen before: *The Quiet Man*, or
The Song of Bernadette. A stranger
in a blue Thames van came from somewhere
to the west as night drew in, to unload
the big, flat cans with reels in them and tramp
up the unpainted stairs to the organ-loft
in the church hall. But I don't remember
seeing this film before: which must be right
because I can't recall what happens next,
or even whether it has a happy ending.

The Dark Room

From all corners of the land they came
to the Poetic Seminary, seldom
from any but the most remote parts,
after the drudgery of crops and cattle
in the cold season of the year.
Assigned a subject, they were locked all night
in a dark room to compose their verse.

In the morning lights were brought so they could
commit their lines to writing. Whereupon
with the publisher's blessing they could go home
to the grace and favour of 'the gentlemen
and rich farmers of the countryside,
by whom they were richly entertained
and made much of'. That is what Bergin says.

I have seen such places even today:
the roadside milk-stand at Gullane, not far
from the stone circle whose radius points
to the sun rising east of Caherbarnagh;
or the Damhscoil at Coolea behind the mountain
where Ó Riada's bees, intent in their darkness,
generate the honey that will bring them praise.

Euryalus

i.m. Mick Imlah

They gathered for the foot-race: at the front, Euryalus
and Nisus, friends from their early childhood.
Euryalus was young and handsome: Nisus,
devoted to him with no thought for himself.
All line up, and, at the starter's shout,
they're off, streaming onward like a fleeting cloud,
eyes on the finish line. Nisus takes the lead,
forging ahead, like the wind, faster than lightning.
Next, but a good way back, comes Salius,
and after him Euryalus, keeping in touch.
Then Helymus of Sicily, and on his heels
the Trojan Diores, shoulder thrust forward;
if the course had been ten yards more, he'd have passed
Helymus, left him for dead. Exhausted,
they're near the end, when the unlucky Nisus
slips on the blood, shed at the sacrifice
and soaking the close-cut grass. Ready
to exult and take the crowd's acclaim,
he skids on the treacherous surface,
loses his balance and crashes face down
on the gruesome blood-steeped racetrack.
But still he won't forget the bonds of love;
reaching up, he impedes Salius,
who also tumbles onto the blood-caked sand.
Euryalus flashes by. Through the intervention
of his fallen friend, he is leading. And soon
he has won, cheered on by fanatical applause.
Salius shouts his anguish at the judges

and to the whole stadium, protesting
that he's been robbed of victory by a foul.
But no one cares about him; Euryalus
has won the hearts of everyone
with his strength and grace, and by the sympathy
his tears provoke: by the power of his youth
just now coming into its own, and made
all the more appealing by his beauty.

One dark night, years later on, the two of them
raided the enemy camp and hacked
the heads from the Rutulian leaders.
Euryalus dressed up in foreign clothes
and put on a shining helmet. The light
glinting from it revealed him. Nisus, hearing
the outcry, doubles back to help him.
But they're doomed. Volcens kills Euryalus,
and Nisus kills him in vengeance.
And then they are all on top of him:
all of them fighting against Nisus on his own
until he lies dead, stretched on Euryalus's body.

Aeneid, V and IX

Menoetes

Turnus, on his side, killed the brothers
who had come from Apollo's lands
in south-west Turkey, and also Menoetes,
a young Arcadian who had always hated war –
for all the good it did him. He'd grown up
in a small house, working as a fisherman
in the rivers around Lerna where the catch
is plentiful, knowing nothing about war
or politics, living in the same district
where his father had farmed his rented land.

Aeneid, XII, 5 17–2 1

The Match Coach

in memory of heroes

I had just, or so I dreamt, moved on ahead
to the bridge where the weeping willow
bows down over the river when I saw
Garry MacMahon running back towards me
out of the mist. 'Hurry on!' he called:
'The coach will leave without you, and you'll miss
the match.' 'Who else is coming?' I asked him,
'Who is already on the bus?' 'John Kerins is there,' he said.
'Tom Creedon will come for certain:
Humphrey Kelleher, Jim Brosnan, Christy Ring,
and Michael McCarthy from O'Donovan Rossa's.'
'I'll come,' I said, 'if you're sure Toots is there.
And tell me one last thing: who is the driver?'
Garry said, 'If it comes to it, I'll drive the bus myself.'

Connolly's Bookshop

It will come to all of us. First close off
the upstairs, blockading it with banks
of books you're not allowed to see, or presumed
to be interested in seeing. Next the shelves
on the back wall where philosophy was.
In due course the languages will go, until
bit by bit you're marooned in the middle
on your high stool amongst the books that show
why books are out of date, why you must move
with the times and be careful what you stock,
defiant Crusoe at the centre of your island.

You Know the Way

You know the way how, crossing Central Park,
trying to get to the West Side from the east
or to the East Side museums from the west,
you stray off line –

I'll start again. You know the way how,
driving into Millstreet, you must decide
at the top of Lislehane whether to go
west to Ballydaly or east by Coalpits –

I'll start one last time: you know the way
how, when you get the Oxford Tube, you
must decide whether to get off at Notting Hill
or stay on till Marble Arch or Victoria –

well, that is how it is at this stage of things:
no right or wrong way, not much turning
on which you choose, or how far the decision
will take you from the straight and narrow.

Specific Gravity

According to Pindar, the best of all things
is water. Next to it everything
seems less. So I've carried grief to the clifftop
behind the Connor Pass where the density
of a low sky meets the sea. What gives our species
its comparative weight, I wonder, as I watch
the sun feeling for cloud-gaps to direct
its beams on the small lakes inland which look
like inky scraps of crêpe dropped on a table:
a child's trick. And, as the days since her death
turn to weeks, the weeks to months, the sea wind
might drain all trace of fluid from the eyes.

Procne

This year, she's back to me again at night,
the swallow that alights on the porch roof
to practise her elegy: distraction
from sleep, or from a breakthrough composition,
like the swallow that Queen Gunnhild sent
to disturb the inventive flow of Egill
as he shaped his life-saving poem before dawn.

Or as another swallow troubled Pandarus
and kept him from his life-enhancing business
of bringing the young lovers to each other.
She operates so differently through the day,
you'd never suspect her machinations
in the darkness. Mine swings in deep arcs
around the yard, getting up the courage

and the speed for her high-jumper's plunge
into the shed through the narrow gap left
in the rusting galvanise. Safely nested there,
she attends to her own business, undisturbed
by the ageless obligation of recalling
what happened to her violated sister
and keeping alive the memory of shame.

The Raven's Portion

and the corbeles fee they kest in a greve
– Sir Gawain and the Green Knight

Before they were certain he was well
and truly dead, they kept their distance
and the dogs crouched low in the bushes.
The spies trained their binoculars on him,
watching his cuticles, knowing that nails
don't go on growing after death,
but it's the frail flesh that shrinks. So they'd wait
until the robin landed on the hero's shoulder.
The dogs would get their fair share of the kill
once they'd pulled out the last piece of gut
to throw it in the bushes for the raven
who'd wheeled in expectation all day long,
impassive, cold, detached, embedded, high,
knowing he'll get his portion in the end.

At the Hallé

He sat by her side, near the front, sideways on
to the cellos and the second violins
under the gold blazon of the brass section.
He feared she'd see if he risked a sideways glance,
hoping for some imperfection that would mean
he was not so totally outclassed:
her nose slightly too big; the small blemish
on her left cheek (the right as you looked at it)
which you could only see when you enlarged
her image on the computer screen.
Around her eyes, he knew, were thin, tired lines,
and under them were deeper lines – 'bags' even –
under the right eye in particular.

He knew that in due course a time would come
when he would take no such satisfaction
in looking for her blemishes and would wonder
if he might have done better for himself.

But he was still far from that time yet,
as he looked straight ahead, taking comfort
in his full appreciation of the harmonies.

On Being Late

for Josie

She never shows up early, out of fear
of being first and having to stand silent
in good time. But there are dangers:
of being shut out of the Buddhist centre,
ringing a vain bell; or like Setanta,
set upon alone outside the gate
by the fierce hound of Culann, and then fated
forever to stand guard in all weathers.
Or the late wedding guest who was less welcome
than the vagrants on the roadside byways.
Older, we live in fear of being late,
for events, appointments, trains. Because
there will be a time when we will all be late
and it won't matter whether we come at all.

And Spoil the Child

An upright man – a man I learned things from,
a man I even in many ways admired –
swung a stick high in the air, to bring it down
after one or two preparatory swishes
and a light upward clip on the fingertips
of the right hand supported at the wrist
of Barty, a hopeless speller – with such force
and rage that the boy's bare feet danced a tattoo
and jiggled on the floor as if he stood
on the burning pavement of Hell's judgement.

Enif

Fairly marginal, even to the shape
of Pegasus, but seven thousand times
brighter than our sun, that busy old fool,
it is the perfect figure for that love
or hang-up, desperation or obsession,
so distant now: but in its time so hot
that, if you were near it, all kindly forms
of life would burn in an instant, more utterly
than the wood-insect that falls onto
the black-hot surface of the kitchen range.

The Thaw

She said there was a thaw in our relations,
which meant (or so it then seemed to me)
that what before had been the sheerest white
and silent and moon-hard glistening
was now no better than a yielding slush
that we could make our sorry passage through.

Against such petty warmth I raise my hand
and beg: return our human cold again
so, packed in ice, we can retain whatever
it was we once must have meant by love
and the kind frost that stopped it going off.

Robbing the Orchard

Her house was hardly more than fifty yards
from the old school by the bridge
and it was easy to run away. Though nothing
is left of the school now but a single wall
marked by ivy patterns, you can still think you hear
the cries of pain inflicted by her brother,
the old-style sadist teacher, as we scurried
back across the ditch with the stolen apples.

We only saw her once, waving her stick
and calling, 'When the fine weather comes
I'll get new clothes in town and go to all
your houses and complain you to your fathers.
You can be sure I will.' We went there last week
with the half-hope of giving something back:
to hang apples back on the trees, stunted
and choked by wintergrass as they were now.

But we found no bough with strength enough to bear
even a crab apple, fighting a lost cause
amid the bitter green and bullying elders.

Out of Sync

Sarah Broom

Just as we can't picture to our satisfaction
the faces of those dearest to us
in their absence but still know they're somewhere,
your bulletins put us, all of us, off the scent:
those positive reports from a journalist
embedded deep behind enemy lines.
We'd all got into the way of thinking
that, in spite of everything, you'd still be there
always. Yes, you would be ill, and your body
agonised by strategies and trials.
But you would still always be there.

Until, last night at midnight while we slept
on our garden watch, you were buried –
body and heart and mind – at eleven
in the morning on your side of the world.
So we must try a different way
of bringing you to mind and holding you
without the prompts that you provided.
We are left now to find out on our own
how this new order of things can be envisaged.

Sawdust

The big top was put up inside the gate
of the town park, where the funeral home is now.
That rain-soaked Easter it was hardly dry enough;
but after deliberation they went ahead,
laying straw along the walkways through
the canvas awning. Despite the sawdust,
the horses threw up a dark spray of mud
on the flinching children in row one.

After the trapeze artists, sinful, high and daring,
and the clowns who fell around and burst balloons,
they asked for seven big men as volunteers
while the strong man rubbed sawdust on his hands.
He lay on his back, supine, and they placed
a long plank on his upraised soles. The hard men
climbed on: Mister O; John Sing; the big drummer
from the pipers' band. The others I didn't know.

The ringmaster called for silence and the drums
beat menacingly. Slowly, miraculously,
the plank began to shudder upwards
from the ground. Then we heard a crack echo
like a stick snapping in a wood. The men
tumbled in all directions, and hopped back
over the low rails. The strong man was wrapped
in a starry blanket and they hurried him out the side.

The clowns came back, and after them the horses.
They started to assemble the huge cages
for the lions, with warnings to be careful.
They gave the children buns to hold out to the elephant.
But they never told us what happened to the strong man.

Dublin Bay

To begin with, tight knots, dark bruises
the colour of drying, hardening blood.
So where does that flare of folded red
come from, that parachute silk
of layered satin, bedsheet or nightdress,
petals so much at the mercy
of the next south-westerly that blows?

Evacuee

my Manchester mother

Raincoats unbelted, socks up to their knees,
in films of the first weeks of the War,
boys and girls of eight or ten march bravely
to their placements in the countryside,
escaping bombs expected in the city.

Having, too, escaped from the threatened city,
she had woken up in those same weeks
every morning to birdsong and the calling
of calves, thinking, she told us later,
that things would always be idyllic from now on.

But when one day she woke to hear the rain
beating like gunfire on the eastern windows
as the wind urged it onward, and she thought
of those children picking their way to school
on wet Manchester cobbles before they went,

each with their brown-paper parcel of clothes and food,
out to uncomforting places in the country
where they cried themselves to sleep, far from friends
and from parents stumbling down to the shelters,
she wished that, after all, she too could go home.

The Mantuans

When a game of dice has reached its end,
the person who has lost stands there alone,
and throws the dice again to see what went wrong,

while the crowd jostles round the winner:
one runs in front, another plucks at his back,
a third seeks his attention from the side.

He doesn't stop, greeting this one and that;
whoever he shakes hands with is content,
and so he manages to disengage himself.

So it was with me in that dense throng,
turning my face to them, one side, then the other,
and escaping from them by my promises . . .

'But see how that spirit, standing there apart,
all on its own, is looking over at us;
it will point out the quickest way to go.'

We came up to it. O Lombard spirit,
how remote and disdainful you were standing,
and in your eyes' movements noble, unhurried.

It said nothing whatsoever to us,
letting us pass, in the manner of a lion
just watching us from where it crouches.

But Virgil drew alongside it, asking
that it show us the best way to climb upwards;
but the spirit just ignored what he requested.

Instead it asked about our homeland and our lives.
And when my gracious guide began his answer
'Mantua' . . . the spirit was all attention,

and jumped towards him from its previous station,
saying 'Oh Mantuan, I am Sordello
from your country.' And they embraced each other.

Oh wretched Italy, homeground of misery,
ship with no pilot in a mighty storm,
no queen of your provinces, but a whorehouse.

That noble spirit was as quick as that,
just at the sweet sound of his homeland's name,
to give his fellow citizen such greeting.

And now in you your live inhabitants
can't live without war, and one hacks at another
though enclosed within the same boundary wall.

Search, wretched land, all round the shores
of your sea-coasts, and then say from your heart
if any part of you can boast of peace . . .

Regardless as you are, observe the Montagues
and Capulets, the Monaldi and the Filippeschi,
those already mourning and these in dread . . .

And if I'm allowed to ask, Jove on high
who on the Earth was crucified for us,
are your just eyes turned somewhere else?

Or is this some preparation you are making
in the depths of your wisdom for some good
that is totally shut off from our perception?

For the cities of Italy are all full
of tyrants, and every backwoodsman
who plays the nationalist is a Marcellus.

Oh my Florence. You can indeed feel happy
about this digression, which doesn't touch you,
of course, since your people are so reasonable.

Many have justice in their hearts but release it
slowly because it doesn't come instinctive to the bow.
But your people have it always on their tongues.

Many refuse public responsibility;
but your people don't wait until they are asked,
shouting out eagerly, 'I am ready for it.'

So now rejoice, because you have good reason:
so prosperous, so peaceable, so wise you are.
If I am right, the facts will bear me out.

Athens and Sparta, who made the ancient laws
and were so civic-minded in their customs,
give only the merest hint at life well lived

compared to you who make such good provision
for the winter that what you spin in October
hardly lasts to the middle of November.

How often in the time still in your memory
have you changed laws, currency, offices
and practices, and replaced the leadership.

And if you remember and still see any light,
you will see how you resemble that sick woman
who can't find any comfort in her bed
but tries to ease her pain by tossing and turning.

Dante, Purgatorio, canto 6

The Seasons of Cullen Church

I wondered how anyone could ever imagine unquiet
slumbers for the sleepers in that quiet earth.
       – EMILY BRONTË, *Wuthering Heights*

I

Angels on permanent watch: the first holding
the white font inside the door, eyes down
so as not to embarrass you as you dipped
a reverent finger, catching no one's eye.
Two marking the high altar's borders.

II

August mornings and the cycle past the field-dew –
Drop down dew, ye Heavens, from above –
on the way to serve Mass
for the visiting priests: natives returned
from California, Manchester or the Far East.

III

The dark week before Easter when you practised
for the devotions – *Was ever grief like mine?* –
when the bell had lost its tongue and they struck
together flat wooden clappers, not to betray
the least trace of jubilation.

IV

Benediction, and the small hot tablet
onto which the priest spooned out
the tea-like incense, then to swing
the thurible and throw onto the air
the rich smell of death and consolation.

V

Snow at New Year: walking down to Mass
for the Feast of the Circumcision:
Now dismiss me, Lord! Had we, like Simeon,
lived long enough? But that night
the sky over the graveyard frosted with stars.

A Sin of Your Past Life

The rule of the confessional was clear –
that, if you couldn't bring to mind a sin
committed since your last Confession,
you should repeat-confess a sin of your past life
for which you were truly sorry. My sin
was a lie: one summer morning I was walking
to the shop with the dog who, unaccountably,
stopped in the road looking uncertain.
I pleaded with her to come on – 'Bran! Bran!' –
but she just stood and stared. I followed
her home and said there was a bull in the road
we'd been afraid to pass. In later years
I could have rehearsed sin after sin
in thought, word, deed and omission,
but nothing as simply veritable as that.
Bless me, Father, for I have sinned.
A hand cross-gestures through the dim-lit grille:
Say three Hail Marys. Pray for me, my child.

Stigmata

The last things of all were his chapped hands
folded across his chest in the city morgue
where he lay with rosary beads (not his) woven
between his fingers, and her loud cry
'Those cursed turnips!', because of the endless
winter mornings when, hail, rain, or sleet,
a north wind and a cast-iron knife
conspired to crack the soft skin
that now would never ever heal again.

Swifts

We'd started to fear they might not come at all
as May lapsed into June and the roads
stayed free of all their diving clamour
when, suddenly, they were there – no pace perceived,
like unexplained gifts on Christmas morning,
or the presence of the returning swallows
that Eoghaneen watched for every spring,
or the shearwaters who were all around us
one mystic Skellig midnight, souls returned
from their other, closed life deep out at sea.

As if the Hare

But if I always seem to be returning
to those few fields, few years of long ago
as if there'd been nothing in the interim,
this only happened yesterday. We walked
by Julia's well in the fading light and saw
a hare come up the road towards us, till
he was a few yards off. He scuffed the ground,
half-turned sideways, affecting indifference
as if what people thought meant nothing to him,
as if absorbed in writing his own message
in the dust. And then he deigned to see us,
still as we were, ten feet away, and, turning
in no great hurry, he loped into the field
through the gap we'd made there in the 'fifties.
Then we ran too, to gaze down the furzy glen.

Meeting in the Small Hours

He was there again in the small hours:
not this time in a dream, but in a dream
of dreaming. Even so the two of us
looked aside, stuck for something to discuss
that was not a matter of life and death,
so we fell back on football and the elections.

Then suddenly he started talking: talking
as he'd never talked in his life. He knew
it wasn't wise to take up cigarettes again
at the wedding the day before; and driving back
the engine misfired once, or twice. And then
I started talking too. I told him about

two other recurrent dreams: the first that I
was smoking again too, but it was all right
because I knew I could give up. Stranger than that,
my twilight dream of the car headlights failing –
but that too was all right because I knew
they'd work again. Then his expression changed:

I watched him brush a small worm of ash
from his jacket. 'Time to go back,' he said.
'And I don't know if I will get away again.'

The Boat

i.m. Seamus Heaney

Take the case of a man in a boat
in deep water. The wind and the waves
and the craft's tossing cause him to stumble
if he makes to stand up, for, no matter how firmly
he tries to hold on, through the boat's slithering
he bends and he staggers, so unstable
the body is. And yet he is safe.

It's the same with the righteous:
if they fall, they are falling only
like a man in a boat who is safe and sound
as long as he stays within the boat's timbers.

Piers Plowman, passus 8